Snoop Dogg

by Z.B. Hill

Superstars of Hip-Hop

Alicia Keys

Beyoncé

Black Eyed Peas

Ciara

Dr. Dre

Drake

Eminem

50 Cent

Flo Rida

Hip Hop:
A Short History

Jay-Z

Kanye West

Lil Wayne

LL Cool J

Ludacris

Mary J. Blige

Notorious B.I.G.

Rihanna

Sean "Diddy" Combs

Snoop Dogg

T.I.

T-Pain

Timbaland

Tupac

Usher

Snoop Dogg

by Z.B. Hill

Mason Crest

Snoop Dogg

Mason Crest
370 Reed Road
Broomall, Pennsylvania 19008
www.masoncrest.com

Printed and bound in the United States of America.

First printing
9 8 7 6 5 4 3 2 1

Library of Congress Cataloging-in-Publication Data

Hill, Z. B.
  Snoop Dogg / by Z.B. Hill.
     p. cm. – (Superstars of hip hop)
  Includes index.
  ISBN 978-1-4222-2515-8 (hard cover) – ISBN 978-1-4222-2508-0 (series hardcover) – ISBN 978-1-4222-9217-4 (ebook)
 1. Snoop Dogg, 1972–-Juvenile literature. 2. Rap musicians–United States–Biography–Juvenile literature. I. Title.
  ML3930.S68H55 2012
  782.421649092–dc23
  [B]
                          2011019653

Produced by Harding House Publishing Services, Inc.
www.hardinghousepages.com
Interior Design by MK Bassett-Harvey.
Cover design by Torque Advertising & Design.

Publisher's notes:
- All quotations in this book come from original sources and contain the spelling and grammatical inconsistencies of the original text.
- The Web sites mentioned in this book were active at the time of publication. The publisher is not responsible for Web sites that have changed their addresses or discontinued operation since the date of publication. The publisher will review and update the Web site addresses each time the book is reprinted.

DISCLAIMER: The following story has been thoroughly researched, and to the best of our knowledge, represents a true story. While every possible effort has been made to ensure accuracy, the publisher will not assume liability for damages caused by inaccuracies in the data, and makes no warranty on the accuracy of the information contained herein. This story has not been authorized nor endorsed by Snoop Dogg.

Contents

Hip-Hop lingo

Poverty is when people are poor and cannot take proper care of themselves.

'Hood is another way to say neighborhood. It's usually used in cities.

A **charity** is a group that gives time, money, or other things to help make people's lives better.

Chapter 1

Big Snoopy D.O. Double-Gizzle

Snoop Dogg stands on a stage in London. Huge crowds of people surround him. The July air is warm. Snoop and other artists have gathered to send a message to the world—**poverty** must end! And who better to send this message than Snoop? He is, in his own words, "the President of the United Ghettos of the World, Big Snoopy D.O. Double-Gizzle!"

Here was Snoop Dogg, being a leader. This man, who was once just a skinny kid from California, had become a true hip-hop star. He'd been through a lot in his life. But somehow it made him want to help other people.

Live 8

The event was called Live 8. It took place on July 2, 2005. The idea was to have eight concerts in eight cities. Seems simple, right? But here's the catch—the eight concerts happened at the same time! All over the world, people got together to send a message to world leaders—poverty in Africa must end.

Live 8 asked Snoop to perform because of his fame. People look up to him. And because of artists like Snoop, Live 8 was a success. Snoop felt very strongly about doing the concert. While on stage, he said:

> "America is one place where you can go from nothing to something. I come from the **'hood** in Long Beach, and now, I'm a boss of the entertainment industry. It feels good to be working with Live 8 to share the same opportunity for progress with my people in Africa. So don't forget to make the choice to change the world."

Snoop Dogg poses with an Iraq war veteran who was helped by the Fisher House Foundation, July 2005. Snoop performed at the Salute to the Troops charity event in Honolulu, Hawaii, which raised money for Fisher House.

Live 8 did raise a lot of money for Africa. But Snoop's **charity** work didn't end there.

Support Our Troops

Later that month, Snoop went to Hawaii. He went there to support American troops. He performed at an event to raise money for soldiers who had been hurt. He led the crowd in call-and-response songs. He got them to sing along. He even had some of them dancing. It was a great way to bring joy to the men and women there. They had served their country. Now Snoop was trying to give them back something in return.

None of it could have happened without hip-hop. Over almost twenty years, Snoop built a hip-hop empire. Like so many hip-hop stars, he started with nothing. Today, people around the world know his face and his style.

So how did it all begin?

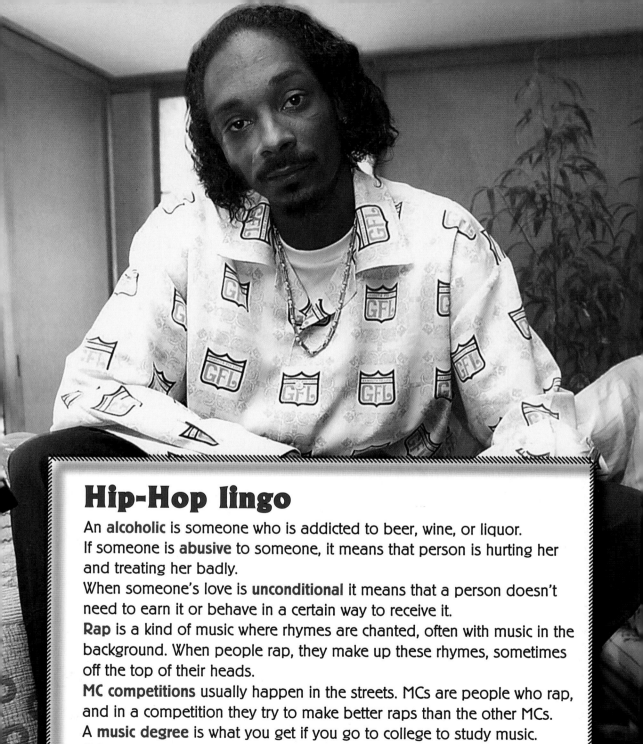

Hip-Hop lingo

An **alcoholic** is someone who is addicted to beer, wine, or liquor.

If someone is **abusive** to someone, it means that person is hurting her and treating her badly.

When someone's love is **unconditional** it means that a person doesn't need to earn it or behave in a certain way to receive it.

Rap is a kind of music where rhymes are chanted, often with music in the background. When people rap, they make up these rhymes, sometimes off the top of their heads.

MC competitions usually happen in the streets. MCs are people who rap, and in a competition they try to make better raps than the other MCs.

A **music degree** is what you get if you go to college to study music.

A **feud** is a fight between two people or groups that goes on a long time.

Growing Up in the LBC

Snoop's real name is Calvin Cordozar Broadus. He was born on October 20, 1971, in Long Beach, California. (Long Beach, California, is also called "the LBC.") No one really knows where the nickname "Snoop Dogg" came from. One story goes that his parents thought he looked like Snoopy. However it happened, the name stuck. From very early on, he was Snoop.

Snoop's Mama

Snoop's mother has an interesting story. Her name is Beverly Broadus Green. Beverly's family is from Mississippi. Her mom grew up very poor, and her mom's dad was a violent man. He was an **alcoholic**. Her mom got tired of his drinking and chose to move the family to Long Beach.

So Beverly grew up in Long Beach. In high school, she fell in love with Vernell Varnado. Vernell is the father of Snoop's older brother, Jerry. Beverly and Vernell broke up after he joined the army.

In 1970, Beverly married Al Cordozar Broadus. But then Vernell came home from the army. He visited Beverly, and they fell in love again. She became pregnant with Vernell's child. She was still married to Al Broadus, so she decided to keep the baby's real father a

Snoop Dogg is pictured here with his mother Beverly Broadus. She is carrying Snoop's young son, Corde. Snoop credits his mother for instilling in him the confidence to succeed in the hip-hop world.

secret. She called him Calvin. Until Al died in 1984, both he and Calvin (Snoop) thought Al was his real father. Later, Beverly had a third and final baby called Bing.

Beverly was a good mother, but she had problems with men. She went through boyfriend after boyfriend. None lasted, and some were mean or **abusive** to Beverly, Calvin, and his brothers.

Life in the LBC

The Broadus family saw hard times while Snoop was a kid. They lived in the eastern part of Long Beach. It was the scene of a lot of drugs and crime. In fact, most of the crime occurred because of drugs. Shootings happened on a regular basis. Snoop's house was not a safe place. His family lived in poverty, and his mother struggled with alcohol and drug addiction.

Snoop tried to help out by making some money. He sold candy, delivered newspapers, and bagged groceries. His life wasn't easy. But he still remembers it as a happy time. In the book about his life, called *Tha Doggfather*, he writes:

> "Most of the memories I have growing up aren't a whole lot different from the ones you've got. Kids are kids and they mostly are wanting and needing and hoping for the same kind of things no matter what side of the tracks they call home."

Snoop's Influences

As a kid, Snoop stayed close to his mom. She was the only constant in his life. Despite her own problems, Beverly gave him **unconditional** love and support. He writes in *Tha Doggfather:*

> "The earliest memories I have are of my mama's loving me, holding me close, kissing my face and stroking my head and making me feel

safe and secure and special in a way that only your mama can. Because of her, and her alone, there was never a time that I went without, never a minute when I didn't believe that I could do anything I put my heart and mind to, never a doubt that I had what it took to make something of myself."

Beverly taught Snoop to be his own person. She told him to try new things and be brave. She believed that her sons would succeed. Snoop writes, "What my mama told me, every day of my life, was that she had faith in me, all the way."

Beverly worked very hard to support her sons. She took two jobs. She cleaned a nursing home and served food in a school cafeteria. But she still found time to take care of her boys. She often made little Snoop's favorite dish: chicken wings and mac'n'cheese.

She was also very religious. She tried to pass on her beliefs to her kids. Every Sunday and Tuesday, the whole family went to Trinity Baptist Church. She even made Snoop sing in the church choir. Believe it or not, this is where Snoop's career started! This is where he found music for the first time. He also learned a lot about his mom's faith at church:

"She had a one-on-one connection to God, a way of talking with Him like He was in the same room or on the phone line, a free and easy flow, passing the time with her closest friend. She *knew* God heard her prayers, knew it like she knew her own face in the mirror, and passed that confidence along to us, making sure we understood that, whatever might be lacking in a father, God would make up for and then some."

Beverly's faith gave her family strength. Snoop writes that he and his brothers never felt unloved. "Mama loved us. God loved us. Nothing else mattered," Snoop wrote in *Tha Doggfather*.

Music in the Blood

Like faith, music was in little Snoop's blood. He never knew his real dad, Vernell Varnado, but Vernell was a musician. He made music for most of his life. He never became famous, but he kept doing it because he loved it.

His mother noticed that Snoop liked music, too. So she made him play piano and sang along as he played. Snoop also remembers listening to his mom's albums from the 1970s. He heard artists

Rappers Warren G (left), Snoop Doggy Dogg (center), and Nate Dogg (right) perform during the Rock the Vote Bus Tour. During the early 1990s the three rappers performed as 213, a group named after the area code for their homes in Long Beach, California.

15

like Johnnie Taylor, the Dramatics, and Curtis Mayfield. Snoop gives his mom credit for his musical career. She made sure music was a big part of her son's life.

It seemed natural for him to make music on his own. He was in sixth grade when he made his first **rap**, called "Super Rhymes." By the time he was 15, Snoop was a well-known rapper in his neighborhood. He often won the freestyle **MC competitions** at school and on the streets.

His friend Warren G was with him most of the time. Warren was a rapper too, and he and Snoop became close friends. They needed each other, because no one else really cared about rap. They both got a job selling candy door-to-door in rich neighborhoods. Finally, they had time to practice their skill. Snoop writes, "G and I would try out raps on each other during those long afternoons walking rich white streets, flowing on anything and everything we could think of."

Rap attracted lots of poor kids. It felt easier to access than other styles of music. Rap was music for the streets. Anyone could pick it up and try it out. As Snoop writes, "If you think you got what it takes, there's nothing stopping you from giving it a shot. You don't need a **music degree**, or ten years of saxophone lessons or a forty-eight-track studio to bust a move."

Things were going well for the young rapper. He had talent. But then he made a bad decision. He joined a gang called the Crips. They were famous for their **feud** with another gang, the Bloods. Snoop wasn't always sure he liked the gang. But it made him feel like he was part of a family. Plus, the gang had other bonuses. It gave Snoop respect and money. And he really wanted both of those things.

But the fun couldn't go on forever. Gang life means selling drugs and doing violent things. Soon, the police caught up with Snoop.

Prison Life

In 1990, Snoop was caught selling crack cocaine. He had just graduated from high school when he went to jail for the first time. While behind bars, Snoop rapped for the other inmates. They told him he was too talented to be in jail. Snoop finally saw that selling drugs was a waste of his life. He decided to change his ways when he got out. Later in his life, Snoop looked back on his drug-selling days with shame. He said that no kids should follow in those footsteps.

When Snoop got out of jail, he got serious about rap. While he was locked up, his best friend Warren G had sent him letters. Together, they kept each other positive and looking to the future. It was a good thing that they did. Because when Snoop got out of jail, he was closer than ever to his dreams.

Hip-Hop lingo

A **mixtape** is a collection of a few songs put on a CD or given away for free on the Internet without being professionally recorded.

A **record label** is a company that produces music for singers and groups and puts out CDs.

A song is called **danceable** if people like to dance to it.

Lyrics are the words in a song.

An album goes **platinum** when it sells more than 1,000,000 copies.

A **tour** means to travel around and play music for people at concerts.

To **protest** something is to go against it in a way that everyone can see.

Critics are people who point out what is wrong with something.

From Ghetto to Superstar

Snoop and his friends had a name for their rap group. They called themselves 213, the area code for the LBC. When Snoop got out of prison, 213 started work on a **mixtape**. Before long, they were selling it out of the trunk of a car. In a few days, they sold over 500 copies! Their friends and people from the 'hood liked 213's sound. But did 213 have what it took to make it big?

Hip-Hop and Gangsta Rap

Hip-hop hasn't been around forever. In fact, it's a pretty new kind of music. The hip-hop that people know today began in the 1970s. But it was changing quickly with the times. By the mid-1980s, a new sound had formed. It came out of the poorest places in America. It came from places where drugs, gangs, and violence ruled the streets. Young people looked around them and wrote what they saw. They called it gangsta rap.

From the start, people had mixed feelings about gangsta rap. Sometimes it seemed to treat really bad things as if they were normal. It made violence and drug use seem not only normal but also cool. A lot of people felt that kids shouldn't listen to gangsta rap.

On the other side, some said gangsta rap was like any other music. They said rappers just told their life stories. They rapped about stuff that really happened. These people argued that gangsta rap didn't say violence and drug use was okay. It simply told the truth.

Father of Gangsta Rap

Warren G had a half-brother named Andre Young, better known as Dr. Dre. Dre took the lead in bringing gangsta rap to the hip-hop world. His group N.W.A. (Niggaz With Attitude) was the first famous gangsta rap group.

Dre is very talented. He's made a lot of good music by himself. But maybe his greatest skill is finding other young talents. He's good at discovering gifted rappers and helping them make albums. In 1991, he teamed up with another rap star, Suge Knight, to start a **record label.** They called it Death Row Records. It became one of the most well-known rap labels.

Dr. Dre has a good ear for hot new music. So when Warren G came to him with one of 213's mixtapes, he agreed to listen. He liked what he heard. He especially liked one of the voices on the tape. It was smooth and laid back. It stood out from the all the others. It was the voice of a young man named Snoop Dogg.

Working Together

Dre and Snoop were a great team. They worked together to make a song for a film called *Deep Cover*. It was the first time the larger world heard Snoop's voice. Right away, people noticed something special. Dre had found a valuable partner in Snoop.

In 1992, Dre asked Snoop to rap on his album called *The Chronic*. Snoop and Dre recorded all over L.A. that year. They realized

Dr. Dre began his career as a rapper and producer with the influential group N.W.A, whose groundbreaking 1989 album *Straight Outta Compton* helped define the genre known as "gangsta rap." Dissatisfied with his record label, Dre formed Death Row with Marion "Suge" Knight.

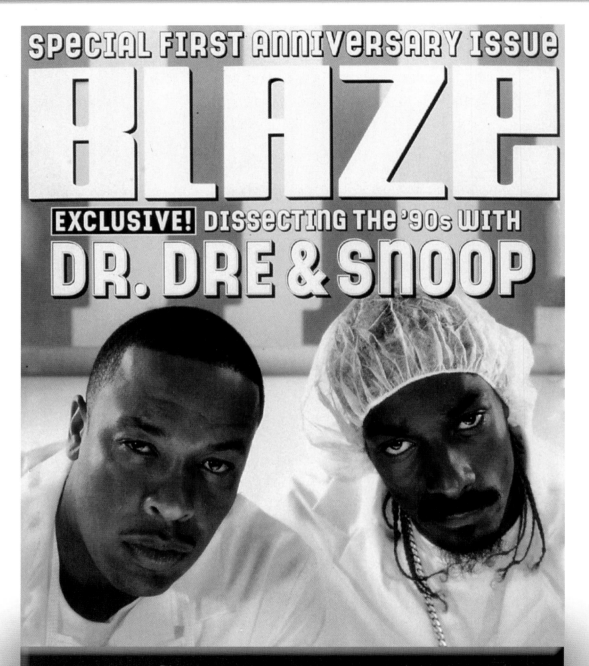

SPECIAL FIRST ANNIVERSARY ISSUE

BLAZE

EXCLUSIVE! DISSECTING THE '90s WITH

DR. DRE & SNOOP

This issue of *Blaze* magazine from 1999, marking its first anniversary, features Dr. Dre and Snoop Dogg. In the magazine's lead article, Dr Dre and Snoop Dogg are credited with shaping the sound of hip-hop in the 1990s.

they were making something fresh. The music they made was both **danceable** and gangsta. They called it G-funk, or gangsta-funk.

G-funk took a flowing, lazy sound and added gangsta **lyrics**. It was a strange combo. Dre and Snoop poured out songs about violence and drugs over a funk beat. It was risky, but it worked.

Sky's the Limit

The Chronic was a huge success. It went **platinum** three times! *The Chronic* did what no gangsta rap album had done so far. It made gangsta rap popular. Kids in white, middle-class neighborhoods listened to it. College students spun it at their house parties. It crossed the line from music for black people to music for everybody.

Good days followed for Snoop. His name wasn't on the album, but he got credit just the same. Everyone knew that *Chronic* wouldn't be anything without Snoop. His laid-back style made the harsh lyrics easier to hear.

As it turned out, those lyrics were a bit too harsh for many people. When Snoop and Dr went on **tour**, women's groups **protested**. They said that some of his words were offensive. Later in life, Snoop agreed with his **critics**. He admits that many of his lyrics do not show women in a healthy way. But he also says that he does not hold the same beliefs as the songs. In his book, he says that in his personal life, he treats women with respect.

Going Solo

After the success of *The Chronic*, it was time for Snoop to go solo. In 1993, he made his first album for Death Row Records, called *Doggystyle*. It was a huge hit. It became the first album in history to hit the charts at number one. It sold over 5 million copies! Snoop was a hip-hop superstar.

Snoop Dogg poses after the 1994 MTV Video Music Awards. He won an award for Best Rap Video for "Doggy Dogg World" from the album *Doggystyle*. The album was Snoop's first to debut at number one on the charts.

Money and fame poured in. Snoop was on the cover of three magazines at once. His music played in every city in America. It was a good time for him. But it had its dangers. Snoop spent money on houses, cars, and long fur coats. He began to worry about all the attention his fame brought him. And he still had ties to the Crips. Snoop wrote, "What had me worried was the fact that, because of my high profile, I was a sitting duck for the ongoing turf war between the Crips and the Bloods."

Hip-Hop lingo

In the court system, an **accomplice** is someone who helps another person commit a crime.

A **manager** is someone who helps and guides a musician.

Royalties are money paid to an artist based on his record sales.

A person's **legacy** is how he is remembered after he dies.

Hard Times

The summer of 1993 was a good one for Snoop. He'd just finished work on *Doggystyle*, and he was about to be a father. Shante Taylor and Snoop had been together since high school. Now she was pregnant with their first baby, a boy named Corde.

Shante and Snoop had something special. They grew up in the same neighborhood. Shante stuck with Snoop even when he went to jail. With Shante, Snoop never had to worry that she was with him for the wrong reasons. She loved him long before he had anything but dreams. Snoop wrote about their special bond:

> "Before I ever even knew I loved her, or ever thought about asking her to be my wife, Shante was my friend, my number one homegirl, and the one person I trusted with my deepest and darkest secrets."

Snoop was having a baby with the woman he loved. And his first solo album was about to come out. Everything was going great until August 24, 1993.

Changed in an Instant

It was a hot sunny day when Snoop almost lost everything. Exactly what happened that day is still not clear. But a man died. Snoop and his bodyguard Malik were both arrested. Malik was charged with murder, and Snoop was charged with being his **accomplice**. Snoop and Lee went on trial, and both were eventually let go. The

Snoop Dogg bows his head in relief after hearing the not-guilty verdict at his murder trial. It was revealed in court that the victim, Philip Woldermariam, had been reaching for his own weapon, and jurors decided the shooting was in self defense.

judge decided that Lee and Snoop had acted in self-defense. But it was a close call. It scared Snoop in a big way. He had been very close to a lifetime in jail. Snoop told *Rolling Stone* magazine:

> "What I've been through has changed me for the better. If I'm gonna come back, I wanna come back right. I'm gonna step up and handle my position, as far as trying to be the role model I tried to deny at the beginning of my career. I was a follower. Now I look at myself as a leader."

Losing a Friend

The hard times kept on coming. In 1996, Snoop lost one of his best friends, rapper Tupac Shakur. At only twenty-five years old, Tupac was already a rap hero. Like Snoop, he was signed to Death Row Records. They became fast friends over a few short years.

Tupac's death hit the entire rap world hard. But it hit Snoop even harder. He'd lost a true friend. Many people in the media held Tupac's death up as an example of the dangerous gangsta life. Snoop didn't have time to agree or disagree. The country had made up its mind: gangsta rap was bad. Sales for gangsta-rap albums dropped.

Hitting Bottom

The hits kept coming. Soon after Tupac's death, Snoop's **manager** sued him. His manager was Suge Knight's wife, Sharitha. She said that Snoop owed her millions of dollars.

It got worse, too. Snoop found out that his label, Death Row, hadn't paid him **royalties** from his albums. They had tried to distract him with cars and jewelry. Meanwhile, they kept the real money for themselves. Snoop was still new to the business. By the time he realized he was being cheated, it was too late.

To make matters worse, his new album, *Tha Doggfather*, wasn't selling very well. After the death of Tupac, people frowned on gangsta rap.

Snoop was broke. It was one of the lowest points in his career. His record label cheated him. He was being sued. Dr. Dre had left Death Row and started a new label. Snoop had no manager. Gang violence made him afraid for his life. And on top of it all, his album wasn't selling. But Snoop wasn't going to give up.

Snoop Dogg (center) poses with fellow Death Row star Tupac Shakur (left) and label cofounder Marion "Suge" Knight (right). Death Row Records, based in Los Angeles, California, had a great success promoting the West Coast "gangsta rap" sound.

After Tupac's death, Snoop Dogg spent a lot of time pondering life and what he wanted to really do with himself. The loss of his friend served as a reminder that he needed to commit himself to the things he really wanted.

Snoop Gets Married

Snoop had a special reason for not giving up: Shante. She never gave up on him either. By 1997, Snoop and Shante had two little boys, Corde and Cordell. The pain that Snoop went through in the early 1990s taught him what was really important in his life. He decided he needed to focus on the family that loved him. So he and Shante got married.

Of course, their marriage wasn't perfect. When you're with a woman you love, Snoop wrote, "sooner or later you'll be waking up to the cold, hard facts that love at first sight doesn't last forever.

What it takes to get through with someone is hanging in, one day at a time, for better or worse, till death do you part."

It hasn't been easy for Snoop and Shante. They have fought a lot. They even got divorced for a few years. But they always seem to find each other again. After all, Shante never stopped supporting her husband. Especially in the hardest times, she was there.

Snoop Dogg and his wife, Shante, have been together since they were young adults living in Long Beach. According to Snoop, the ghetto doesn't teach people what real love is like. He and Shante have been figuring it out the hard way.

Thinking About the Past

Snoop did a lot of thinking around the time of his wedding. He wanted to change his life in more ways than one. He was finally marrying the woman he loved. But what about his career? What about his music?

He thought a lot about Tupac's death. He thought about Tupac's life and **legacy**. He wrote of Tupac:

> "Sometimes, if you're lucky, someone comes into your life who'll take up a place in your heart no one else can fill, someone who's tighter than a twin, more with your than your own shadow, who gets deeper under your skin than your own blood and bones."

Tupac's death made Snoop think about the rap world. He wanted to do something to change it for the better, like Tupac had tried to do. He wanted to take gangsta rap in a new direction. He wrote, "It wasn't enough just to tell it like it is anymore. It was time to tell it like it could be."

THE SOURCE

THE MAGAZINE OF HIP-HOP OLITI

EXCLUSIVE!

SNOOP DOGG

WANTS TO LEAVE DEATH ROW

CAN HE CUT IT ON HIS OWN?

NOTORIOUS
B.
ONE Y
D
DI
DOGG

APRIL
US $2.95 ·

Hip-Hop lingo

A **spokesman** is someone who speaks for a company in public, usually on TV or on the radio.

A **producer** is the person in charge of putting together songs. A producer makes the big decisions about the music.

Satellite radio is a type of radio signal that is bounced off satellites and allows subscribers to receive hundreds of different stations for a fee.

Lupus is a disease that makes the immune system attack the body's own cells and tissue.

Tha Dogg Rises Again

Snoop decided it was time to say goodbye to Death Row. In 1998, he found a new home at No Limit Records. It was time for a fresh start.

No Limit

No Limit Records was a big deal in the late '90s. A smart business-man named Master P owned it. In just three years, he had turned No Limit into a major success. Snoop was in good hands there. He quickly turned out four new albums: *Da Game Is To Be Sold, Not To Be Told*; *Topp Dogg*; *Dead Man Walkin'*; and *Tha Last Meal*.

The albums had okay sales. Some critics said that No Limit had taken the life out of Snoop's songs. They said that No Limit cared more about record sales than Snoop's unique voice. Good or bad, No Limit gave Snoop a steady cash flow. He and Master P surprised everyone when they moved their families into a classy neighborhood outside of Baton Rouge, Louisiana. They were the first black people to live in the rich, all-white neighborhood. They moved there so their kids could grow up somewhere safe with good schools.

From Gangsta to Rich Man

Snoop's move to the suburbs was the start of a major shift in his image. After Tupac died, rap fans began to look for something other than gangsta violence. Plus, Snoop was married and had kids now. He wasn't ready to give up rapping. He needed an image makeover.

This publicity photo was taken around the time that *Paid tha Cost To Be da Bo$$* was released in 2002. In addition to a new musical direction, Snoop began shedding his gangsta image, instead adopting what he called the "pimp" look.

People who had been watching Snoop's career told him he needed to reach out to more people. They said he should change his image to make more fans. So he did, and it worked.

Snoop began to shift from being a "gangsta" to a rich man. In his own words, being rich meant "feeling good, dressing good, and no one's stepping on your alligator shoes." In other words, he was no longer a kid from the streets.

He took that image into his next album, *Paid tha Cost To Be da Bo$$*. He got rid of his baggy blue jeans and do-rags. He began wearing silk suits, alligator shoes, and long fur coats. He tricked out his Cadillac with TV screens and fur-lined seats. He even drank from a special "Snoop" cup, covered in jewels.

Planet Snoop

The new Snoop was a big success. His record sales began to go up as his image became less hardcore. More and more people saw Snoop as someone whose music they could enjoy. Soon big companies wanted Snoop to be their **spokesman**.

He was happy to do TV commercials for cell phones, juice drinks, and video games. Snoop Dogg became a brand all his own. His biggest deal came when MCA records asked him to start his very own label: Doggystyle Records. He started **producing** other rappers that he found fresh and interesting.

Rap music became only one slice of the Snoop Dogg pie. He started to act in movies, a longtime dream. He'd had some small acting roles before. Now he got parts in major films. In 2001, he was in *Training Day* with one of the greats, Denzel Washington.

Top Dogg

In the past few years, Snoop has grown into a wiser man. He still makes mistakes, but he always picks himself back up. One of his mistakes was his divorce. In 2004, he filed for divorce from his wife, Shante. But he quickly changed his mind. He realized his mistake. He told *Rolling Stone*, "My thing was, I was so demanding and not willing to listen. . . . I just got to come back to being you know, Calvin, and realizing what matters to me most, my wife and kids."

In the meantime, Snoop has stayed as busy as ever. He put out four albums in five years: *Rhythm & Gangsta* (2004), *Tha Blue Carpet Treatment* (2006), *Ego Trippin'* (2008), and *Malice n*

Rappers Sean Combs and Snoop Dogg perform at the 29th annual American Music Awards in Los Angeles, January 2002. Snoop is holding the rhinestone-encrusted goblet that he started using at public appearances as part of his new image.

Wonderland (2009.) In 2010, Snoop also rapped a verse on Katy Perry's hit "California Gurls."

In March, 2011, Snoop Dogg released his next album, *Doggumentary*. The album featured Wiz Khalifa, Kanye West, John Legend, and many others. Snoop even recorded a song with country star Willie Nelson. The album hit number 8 on the billboard charts in its first week. In the fall of 2011, Snoop and Wiz Khalifa's "Young, Wild, and Free" became a hit.

Snoop Dogg didn't slow down at that. In February 2012, Snoop announced the title of his next album. He told fans on twitter that his next album was called *Reincarnated*. To be reincarnated means "to come back to life as someone or something else." Fans couldn't wait for the Snoop's 12th album!

Radio Star

Snoop kept pushing his career. In 2004, he started a show for XM **satellite radio**. He chose music that he liked and played it for listeners. The show was a hit, so XM producers asked Snoop to host an entire hip-hop channel, called The Rhyme. It was a perfect fit for Snoop. He handpicked songs and brought in a lot of listeners for XM. Before he started The Rhyme, he said, "I will play music that people have never heard and music that they haven't heard in a long time."

The Big Screen

Snoop has continued to seek out acting roles. He's worked hard to remake his movie image. Like his musical self, movie-star Snoop needed a facelift. He's worked hard to get a lot of different types of roles. He doesn't want to be pegged as just one kind of actor. He's done big-name movies like *Starsky and Hutch*, and he even starred in his own film, *Soul Plane*.

Snoop Dogg arrives at the premiere of Soul Plane with his two sons, Corde and Cordell, also called Spanky and Lil' Snoop. In recent years Snoop Dogg has changed some of his behaviors, in an attempt to set a better example for his sons.

Coach and Father

Lately, Snoop has taken great pride in his kids. He is the head coach of his son's football team, the Rowland Heights Raiders. He loves the team and goes to every practice and every game. When the player won a big game, he gave them their very own team bus. And yes, it was custom built, Snoop-Dogg-style.

Snoop truly enjoys being a coach. He told *Access Hollywood*, "I see how these kids really love me. They love the person, not Snoop Dogg the rapper, but the person who can actually teach them small things in football that might become big things later on in life."

Fighting For His Family

When Snoop's daughter was six years old, he and Shante noticed that something was wrong with her. She had rashes on her skin and her hair was falling out. The doctors told Snoop and his wife that their daughter, Cori, had **lupus**. Since that day, Snoop and Shante have been amazed by their daughter's bravery. Snoop told Eurweb.com about his daughter, "She's the toughest little thing I've ever met. She's on the honor roll, playing volleyball and soft-ball, living life. She has all this joy. In the beginning lupus was winning. But now Cori is."

Together, the family has fought the disease for over five years. It hasn't been easy, but they have hope for the future. Snoop will continue to rap into the future. But he won't be doing it for himself alone. He'll be fighting for his daughter, his two sons, and his wife, Shante.

1971   Snoop was born Calvin Corozar Broadus on October 20 in Long Beach, California.

1990   Calvin is convicted of possessing crack cocaine, sentenced to one year in the Wayside Jail in Anaheim, California.

1992   Snoop appears on Dr. Dre's soundtrack for the movie *Deep Cover* on the title track.

1993   *The Chronic* goes platinum; Snoop is charged in the killing of Phillip Woldemariam; he releases his debut solo album, *Doggystyle*, produced by Dr. Dre. *Doggystyle* becomes the first debut album in history to hit the music charts at number one, going platinum three times.

1996   Snoop is acquitted of his role in the Woldemariam murder; Tupac Shakur is killed; the album *Tha Doggfather* is released.

1997   Snoop marries high school sweetheart, Shante Taylor.

1998   Snoop splits from Death Row Records and signs with No Limit Records; *Da Game Is To Be Sold, Not To Be Told* is released.

1999   *Tha Doggfather* is published; *No Limit Top Dogg* is released.

2000   Snoop switches from No limit to MCA; *Snoop Dogg Presents Tha Eastsidaz* is released; *Tha Last Meal* is released.

2001   Snoop appears in the horror movie *Bones*.

2002   *Snoop Dogg Presents. . . Doggy Style Allstars Vol. 1* is released; *Paid tha Cost to Be da Bo$$* is released.

2004   Snoop stars in *Soul Plane*; the XM satellite radio show "Welcome to Da Chuuch with Big Snoop Dogg" debuts; *The Hard Way* is released; *R&G (Rhythm & Gangsta): The Masterpiece* is released.

2005   Snoop advocates for the release of death row inmate Stanley Tookie, founder of the Crip street gang; he performs at the Live 8 concert in England to raise awareness of worldwide poverty; he is also made executive producer of XM satellite radio's hip-hop channel, The Rhyme.

2006   Snoop is arrested at London's Heathrow Airport for his involvement in a riot started by members of his entourage.

2008   Snoop's new album, *Ego Trippin'*, is released; he also appears on the Super Bowl.

2009   Snoop Dogg joins the Nation of Islam.

2010   Snoop goes on tour; he also appears in Katy Perry's new hit, "California Girls."

2011   Snoop releases *Doggumentary*, his 11th album.

In Books

Baker, Soren. *The History of Rap and Hip Hop*. San Diego, Calif.: Lucent, 2006.

Comissiong, Solomon W. F. *How Jamal Discovered Hip-Hop Culture*. New York: Xlibris, 2008.

Cornish, Melanie. *The History of Hip Hop*. New York: Crabtree, 2009.

Czekaj, Jef. *Hip and Hop, Don't Stop!* New York: Hyperion, 2010.

Haskins, Jim. *One Nation Under a Groove: Rap Music and Its Roots*. New York: Jump at the Sun, 2000.

Hatch, Thomas. *A History of Hip-Hop: The Roots of Rap*. Portsmouth, N.H.: Red Bricklearning, 2005.

Websites

Current Hip-Hop News
www.allhiphop.com

More Snoop
www.snoopheaven.com

Snoop Dogg's Official Site
www.snoopdogg.com

Snoop on Myspace
www.myspace.com/snoopdogg

Rap News
www.rapweekly.com

Discography
Albums

1993 Doggystyle

1996 The Doggfather

1998 Da Game Is to Be Sold, Not to Be Told

1999 No Limit Top Dogg

2000 Tha Last Meal

2002 Snoop Dogg Presents Doggy Style Allstars Volume 1

Paid Tha Cost to Be da Bo$$

2004 The Hard Way (as part of 213)

R&G (Rhythm & Gangsta): The Masterpiece

2006 The Blue Carpet Treatment

2008 Ego Trippin'

2009 Malice n Wonderland

2011 Doggumentary

Index

About the Author

Z.B. Hill is a an author and publicist living in Binghamton, New York. He has a special interest in adolescent education and how music can be used in the classroom.

Picture Credits